FEDERAL CLOUD COMPUTING STRATEGY

Vivek Kundra
U.S. Chief Information Officer

FEBRUARY 8, 2011

TABLE OF CONTENTS

EXECUTIVE SUMMARY

The Federal Government's current Information Technology (IT) environment is characterized by low asset utilization, a fragmented demand for resources, duplicative systems, environments which are difficult to manage, and long procurement lead times. These inefficiencies negatively impact the Federal Government's ability to serve the American public.

Cloud computing has the potential to play a major part in addressing these inefficiencies and improving government service delivery. The cloud computing model can significantly help agencies grappling with the need to provide highly reliable, innovative services quickly despite resource constraints.

Commercial service providers are expanding their available cloud offerings to include the entire traditional IT stack of hardware and software infrastructure, middleware platforms, application system components, software services, and turnkey applications. The private sector has taken advantage of these technologies to improve resource utilization, increase service responsiveness, and accrue meaningful benefits in efficiency, agility, and innovation. Similarly, for the Federal Government, cloud computing holds tremendous potential to deliver public value by increasing operational efficiency and responding faster to constituent needs.

An estimated $20 billion of the Federal Government's $80 billion in IT spending is a potential target for migration to cloud computing solutions (Appendix 1).[1]

Figure 1: Estimated portion of Federal IT spend able to move to the cloud

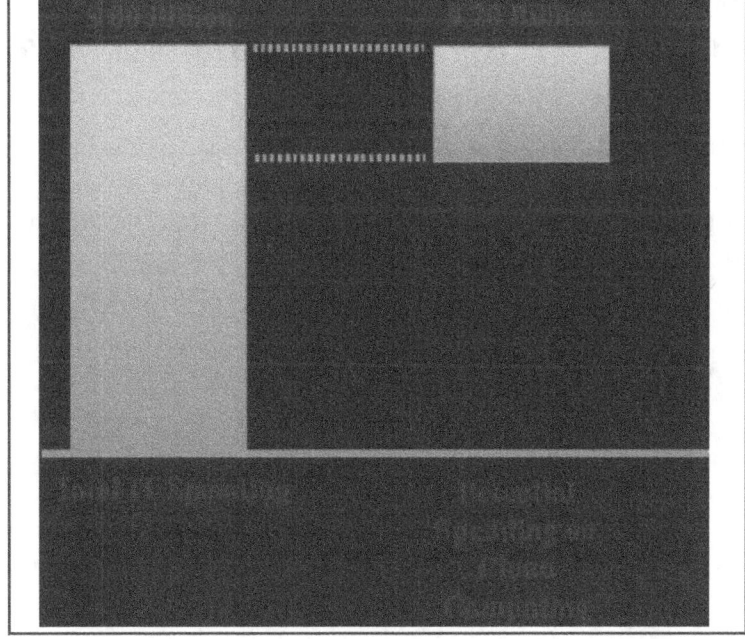

---

1. Based on agency estimates as reported to the Office of Management and Budget (OMB).

To harness the benefits of cloud computing, we have instituted a Cloud First policy. This policy is intended to accelerate the pace at which the government will realize the value of cloud computing by requiring agencies to evaluate safe, secure cloud computing options before making any new investments.

By leveraging shared infrastructure and economies of scale, cloud computing presents a compelling business model for Federal leadership. Organizations will be able to measure and pay for only the IT resources they consume, increase or decrease their usage to match requirements and budget constraints, and leverage the shared underlying capacity of IT resources via a network. Resources needed to support mission critical capabilities can be provisioned more rapidly and with minimal overhead and routine provider interaction.

Cloud computing can be implemented using a variety of deployment models – private, community, public, or a hybrid combination.

Cloud computing offers the government an opportunity to be more efficient, agile, and innovative through more effective use of IT investments, and by applying innovations developed in the private sector. If an agency wants to launch a new innovative program, it can quickly do so by leveraging cloud infrastructure without having to acquire significant hardware, lowering both time and cost barriers to deployment.

This Federal Cloud Computing Strategy is designed to:

- Articulate the benefits, considerations, and trade-offs of cloud computing
- Provide a decision framework and case examples to support agencies in migrating towards cloud computing
- Highlight cloud computing implementation resources
- Identify Federal Government activities and roles and responsibilities for catalyzing cloud adoption

Following the publication of this strategy, each agency will re-evaluate its technology sourcing strategy to include consideration and application of cloud computing solutions as part of the budget process. Consistent with the Cloud First policy, agencies will modify their IT portfolios to fully take advantage of the benefits of cloud computing in order to maximize capacity utilization, improve IT flexibility and responsiveness, and minimize cost.

Figure 2: Cloud benefits: Efficiency, Agility, Innovation

EFFICIENCY	
Cloud Benefits	**Current Environment**
• Improved asset utilization (server utilization > 60-70%) • Aggregated demand and accelerated system consolidation (e.g., Federal Data Center Consolidation Initiative) • Improved productivity in application development, application management, network, and end-user	• Low asset utilization (server utilization < 30% typical) • Fragmented demand and duplicative systems • Difficult-to-manage systems
AGILITY	
Cloud Benefits	**Current Environment**
• Purchase "as-a-service" from trusted cloud providers • Near-instantaneous increases and reductions in capacity • More responsive to urgent agency needs	• Years required to build data centers for new services • Months required to increase capacity of existing services
INNOVATION	
Cloud Benefits	**Current Environment**
• Shift focus from asset ownership to service management • Tap into private sector innovation • Encourages entrepreneurial culture • Better linked to emerging technologies (e.g., devices)	• Burdened by asset management • De-coupled from private sector innovation engines • Risk-adverse culture

I. UNLEASHING THE POWER OF CLOUD

Cloud computing describes a broad movement to treat IT services as a commodity with the ability to dynamically increase or decrease capacity to match usage needs. By leveraging shared infrastructure and economies of scale, cloud computing presents Federal leadership with a compelling business model. It allows users to control the computing services they access, while sharing the investment in the underlying IT resources among consumers. When the computing resources are provided by another organization over a wide-area network, cloud computing is similar to an electric power utility. The providers benefit from economies of scale, which in turn enables them to lower individual usage costs and centralize infrastructure costs. Users pay for what they consume, can increase or decrease their usage, and leverage the shared underlying resources. With a cloud computing approach, a cloud customer can spend less time managing complex IT resources and more time investing in core mission work.

1. Defining cloud computing

Cloud computing is defined by the National Institute of Standards and Technology (NIST)[2] as "a model for enabling convenient, on-demand network access to a shared pool of configurable computing resources (e.g., networks, servers, storage, applications, and services) that can be rapidly provisioned and released with minimal management effort or service provider interaction."[3] NIST has identified five essential characteristics of cloud computing: on-demand service, broad network access, resource pooling, rapid elasticity, and measured service.[4]

Cloud computing is defined to have several deployment models, each of which provides distinct trade-offs for agencies which are migrating applications to a cloud environment. NIST defines the cloud deployment models as follows:

- *Private cloud.* The cloud infrastructure is operated solely for an organization. It may be managed by the organization or a third party and may exist on premise or off premise.

- *Community cloud.* The cloud infrastructure is shared by several organizations and supports a specific community that has shared concerns (e.g., mission, security requirements, policy, and compliance considerations). It may be managed by the organizations or a third party and may exist on premise or off premise.

- *Public cloud.* The cloud infrastructure is made available to the general public or a large industry group and is owned by an organization selling cloud services.

- *Hybrid cloud.* The cloud infrastructure is a composition of two or more clouds (private, community, or public) that remain unique entities but are bound together by standardized or proprietary technology that enables data and application portability (e.g., cloud bursting for load-balancing between clouds).

---

2. http://csrc.nist.gov/groups/SNS/cloud-computing/
3. http://csrc.nist.gov/groups/SNS/cloud-computing/cloud-def-v15.doc
4. http://csrc.nist.gov/groups/SNS/cloud-computing/cloud-def-v15.doc

Cloud computing can also categorized into service models. These are defined by NIST to be:

- *Cloud Software as a Service (SaaS)*. The capability provided to the consumer is to use the provider's applications running on a cloud infrastructure. The applications are accessible from various client devices through a thin client interface such as a web browser (e.g., web-based email). The consumer does not manage or control the underlying cloud infrastructure including network, servers, operating systems, storage, or even individual application capabilities, with the possible exception of limited user-specific application configuration settings.

- *Cloud Platform as a Service (PaaS)*. The capability provided to the consumer is the ability to deploy onto the cloud infrastructure consumer-created or acquired applications created using programming languages and tools supported by the provider. The consumer does not manage or control the underlying cloud infrastructure including network, servers, operating systems, or storage, but has control over the deployed applications and possibly application hosting environment configurations.

- *Cloud Infrastructure as a Service (IaaS)*. The capability provided to the consumer is to provision processing, storage, networks, and other fundamental computing resources where the consumer is able to deploy and run arbitrary software, which can include operating systems and applications. The consumer does not manage or control the underlying cloud infrastructure but has control over operating systems, storage, deployed applications, and possibly limited control of select networking components (e.g., host firewalls).

2. Cloud is a fundamental shift in IT

Cloud computing enables IT systems to be scalable and elastic. End users do not need to determine their exact computing resource requirements upfront. Instead, they provision computing resources as required, on-demand. Using cloud computing services, a Federal agency does not need to own data center infrastructure to launch a capability that serves millions of users.

3. Cloud computing can significantly improve public sector IT

A number of government agencies are adopting cloud technologies and are realizing considerable benefits. For instance, NASA Nebula,[5] through a community cloud, gives researchers access to IT services relatively inexpensively in minutes. Prior to adopting this approach, it would take researchers months to procure and configure comparable IT resources and significant

---

5. http://nebula.nasa.gov/services/
http://nebula.nasa.gov/blog/

management oversight to monitor and upgrade systems. Applying cloud technologies across the entire Federal Government can yield tremendous benefits in efficiency, agility, and innovation. These benefits are described below.

Efficiency improvements will shift resources towards higher-value activities

In FY2010, approximately thirty cents of every dollar invested in Federal IT was spent on data center infrastructure.[6] Unfortunately, only a fraction of this investment delivers real, measurable impact for American citizens. By using the cloud computing model for IT services, we will be able to reduce our data center infrastructure expenditure by approximately 30%[7] (which contributes to the estimated $20 billion of IT spending that could be migrated to cloud computing solutions). Similar efficiency improvements will be seen in software applications and end-user support. These savings can be used to increase capacity or be reinvested in agency missions, including citizen-facing services and inventing and deploying new innovations. Cloud computing can allow IT organizations to simplify, as they no longer have to maintain complex, heterogeneous technology environments. Focus will shift from the technology itself to the core competencies and mission of the agency.

Assets will be better utilized

Across the public and private sectors, data center infrastructure investments are not utilized to their fullest potential. For example, according to a recent survey, many agencies are not fully utilizing their available storage capacity and are utilizing less than 30% of their available server capacity.[8] Low utilization is not necessarily a consequence of poor management, but, instead, a result of the need to ensure that there is reserve capacity to meet periodic or unexpected demand for key functions.

With cloud computing, IT infrastructure resources are pooled and shared across large numbers of applications and organizations. Cloud computing can complement data center consolidation efforts by shifting workloads and applications to infrastructures owned and operated by third parties. Capacity can be provisioned to address the peak demand across a group of applications, rather than for a single application. When demand is aggregated in this fashion and properly managed, the peaks and troughs of demand smooth out, providing a more consistent and manageable demand profile.

As utilization is improved, more value is derived from the existing assets, reducing the need to continuously increase capacity. Fewer machines mean less spending on hardware, software, and operations maintenance, real estate, and power consumption.

Demand aggregation will reduce duplication

The shift to cloud computing can help to mitigate the fragmented data, application, and infrastructure silo issues associated with federated organizational and funding models by focusing on IT services as a utility. IT services become candidates for more cost effective procurement and management, similar to the model currently used for buildings and utility services.

---

6. President's FY2011 Budget
7. Gartner IT Key Metrics Data 2009, Bloomberg, McKinsey analysis
8. Agency Data Center Consolidation Plans submitted to OMB, August 2010

Cloud computing has the potential to provide a more interoperable and portable environment for data and systems. With the appropriate standards, over time, organizations may be able to move to common services and platforms.

Data center consolidation can be accelerated

In February 2010, we launched the Federal Data Center Consolidation Initiative (FDCCI) to consolidate the Federal Government's fragmented data center environment. Through the FDCCI, agencies have formulated detailed consolidation plans and technical roadmaps to eliminate a minimum of 800 data centers by 2015.[9]

Cloud computing can accelerate data center consolidation efforts by reducing the number of applications hosted within government-owned data centers. For those that continue to be owned and operated directly by Federal agencies (e.g., by implementing private IaaS clouds), environments will be more interoperable and portable, which will decrease data center consolidation and integration costs because it reduces unnecessary heterogeneity and complexity in the IT environment.

IT will be simpler and more productive

Cloud computing also provides an indirect productivity benefit to all services in the IT stack. For example, less effort will be required to stand up and develop software testing environments, enabling application development teams to integrate and test frequently in production-representative environments at a fraction of the cost of providing this infrastructure separately.

Agility improvements will make services more responsive

The impact of cloud computing will be far more than economic. Cloud computing will also allow agencies to improve services and respond to changing needs and regulations much more quickly.

With traditional infrastructure, IT service reliability is strongly dependent upon an organization's ability to predict service demand, which is not always possible. For example, the IT system used in the Car Allowance and Rebate System (CARS, more commonly known as "Cash-For-Clunkers") had numerous failures because the load was considerably higher than what its system could handle. The sponsor for "Cash-for-Clunkers," the National Highway Traffic Safety Administration (NHTSA) anticipated a demand of 250,000 transactions over a four month period, but within just 90 days, the system processed approximately 690,000 CARS transactions. Within three days of the first dealer registrations, the system was overwhelmed, leading to numerous outages and service disruptions. The $1 billion appropriated for the program was nearly exhausted within one week and an additional $2 billion dollars was appropriated to triple the potential number of transactions just nine days after the program began. NHTSA deployed a customized commercial application hosted in a traditional data center environment, but the CARS system presented a very good example of an unpredictable service demand and a short development window that could have been more efficiently handled using a cloud computing approach. Cloud computing will allow agencies to rapidly scale up to meet unpredictable demand thus minimizing

---

9. OMB, *25-point implementation plan to reform Federal information technology management*, December 9, 2010, http://www.cio.gov/documents/25-Point-Implementation-Plan-to-Reform-Federal%20IT.pdf

similar disruptions. Notably, cloud computing also provides an important option for agencies in meeting short-term computing needs such as the one above; agencies need not invest in infrastructure in cases where service is needed for a limited period of time.

Services will be more scalable

With a larger pool of resources to draw from, individual cloud services are unlikely to encounter capacity constraints. As a result, government services such as "Cash-for-Clunkers" would be able to more rapidly increase capacity and avoid service outages. Given appropriate service level agreements and governance to ensure overall capacity is met, cloud computing will make the government's IT investments less sensitive to the uncertainty in demand forecasts for individual programs, which frequently emerge rapidly in response to national program needs which cannot be foreseen in the early stages of the Federal budget cycle.

Innovation improvements will rapidly enhance service effectiveness

Cloud computing will not only make our IT services more efficient and agile, it will also serve as an enabler for innovation. Cloud computing allows the Federal Government to use its IT investments in a more innovative way and to more easily adopt innovations from the private sector. Cloud computing will also help our IT services take advantage of leading-edge technologies including devices such as tablet computers and smart phones.

IT innovation has transformed how the private sector operates and revolutionized the efficiency, convenience, and effectiveness with which it serves its customers. In our everyday lives, we can track the status of a shipment; order a pizza or a pair of shoes; make travel, hotel, and restaurant reservations; and collaborate with friends and colleagues – all online, anytime, and anywhere. Yet, when it comes to dealing with the Federal Government, we too often need to stand in line, hold on the phone, or mail in a paper form. For many reasons such as policy and other constraints, the Federal Government has not innovated as quickly as the private sector and has consequently missed out on many of the benefits offered through IT.

Encourage entrepreneurial culture by reducing risk

Cloud-based projects can be conceived, developed, and tested with smaller initial investments than traditional IT investments. Rather than laboriously building data center capacity to support a new development environment, capacity can be provisioned in small increments through cloud computing technologies. After the small initial investment is made, the project can be evaluated for additional investment or cancellation. Projects that show promise can gain valuable insights through the evaluation process. Less promising projects can be cancelled with minimal losses. This "start small" approach collectively reduces the risk associated with new application development. Reducing the minimum required investment size will also provide a more experimental development environment in which innovation can flourish.

II. DECISION FRAMEWORK FOR CLOUD MIGRATION

The broad scope and size of the cloud transformation will require a meaningful shift in how government organizations think of IT. Organizations that previously thought of IT as an investment in locally owned and operated applications, servers, and networks will now need to think of IT in terms of services, commoditized computing resources, agile capacity provisioning tools, and their enabling effect for American citizens. This new way of thinking will have a broad impact across the entire IT service lifecycle – from capability inception through delivery and operations.

The following structured framework presents a strategic perspective for agencies in terms of thinking about and planning for cloud migration.

Figure 3: Decision Framework for Cloud Migration

Select	Provision	Manage

▪ Identify which IT services to move and when
 	
  – Identify sources of value for cloud migrations: efficiency, agility, innovation
 	
  – Determine cloud readiness: security, market availability, government readiness, and technology lifecycle
	▪ Aggregate demand at Department level where possible
	
	▪ Ensure interoperability and integration with IT portfolio
	
	▪ Contract effectively to ensure agency needs are met
	
	▪ Realize value by repurposing or decommissioning legacy assets and redeploying freed resources
		▪ Shift IT mindset from assets to services
		
		▪ Build new skill sets as required
		
		▪ Actively monitor SLAs to ensure compliance and continuous improvement
		
		▪ Re-evaluate vendor and service models periodically to maximize benefits and minimize risks

Framework is flexible and can be adjusted to meet individual agency needs

A broad set of principles and considerations for each of these three major migration steps is presented below. Please refer to Section 3 for an illustration of how these considerations can be applied, using Federal case study examples.

1. Selecting services to move to the cloud

Successful organizations carefully consider their broad IT portfolios and create roadmaps for cloud deployment and migration. These roadmaps prioritize services that have high expected value and high readiness to maximize benefits received and minimize delivery risk. Defining exactly which cloud services an organization intends to provide or consume is a fundamental initiation phase activity in developing an agency roadmap.

The chart shown below uses two dimensions to help plan cloud migrations: *Value* and *Readiness*. The Value dimension captures cloud benefits in the three areas discussed in Section 1 (i.e., efficiency, agility, and innovation). The Readiness dimension broadly captures the ability for the IT service to move to the cloud in the near-term. Security, service and market characteristics, government readiness, and lifecycle stage are key considerations. As shown below, services with relatively high value and readiness are strong candidates to move to the cloud first.

Figure 4: Selecting Services for Cloud Migration

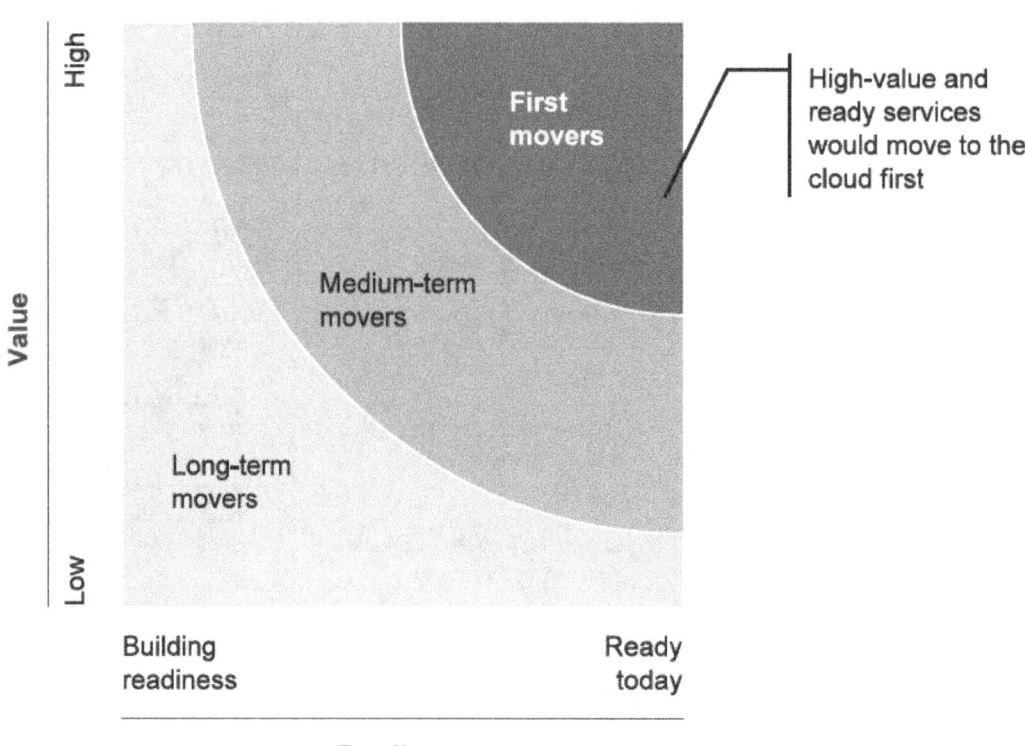

The relative weight of the value and readiness dimensions can be adjusted to meet the individual needs of agencies. Some agencies may stress innovation and security while others may stress efficiency and government readiness. However, the logic and structure of the framework should be applicable for all agencies.

Described below are a number of considerations for value and readiness that agencies may find helpful when completing this evaluation.

Identify sources of value

As described in Section 1, cloud computing provides three primary sources of business value: efficiency, agility, and innovation. Listed below are a number of considerations for each value category.

Agencies should feel free to stress one or more of these sources of value according to their individual needs and mission goals. For instance, some agencies may place a higher value on agility, while others may stress cost savings brought about by greater computing efficiency.

Efficiency: Efficiency gains can come in many forms, including higher computer resource utilization due to the employment of contemporary virtualization technologies, and tools that extend the reach of the system administrator, lowering labor costs. Efficiency improvements can often have a direct impact on ongoing bottom line costs. Further, the nature of some costs will change from being capital investment in hardware and infrastructure (CapEx) to a pay-as-you go (OpEx) model with the cloud, depending on the cloud deployment model being used. Services that have relatively high per-user costs, have low utilization rates, are expensive to maintain and upgrade, or are fragmented should receive a relatively high priority for consideration.

Agility: Many cloud computing efforts support rapid automated provisioning of computing and storage resources. In this way, cloud computing approaches put IT agility in the hands of users, and this can be a qualitative benefit. Existing services that require long lead times to upgrade or increase / decrease capacity should receive a relatively high priority for consideration, and so should new or urgently needed services to compress delivery timelines as much as possible. Services that are easy to upgrade, are not sensitive to demand fluctuations, or are unlikely to need upgrades in the long-term can receive a relatively low priority.

Innovation: Agencies can compare their current services to contemporary marketplace offerings, or look at their customer satisfaction scores, overall usage trends, and functionality to identify the need for potential improvements through innovation. Services that would most benefit from innovation should receive a relatively high priority.

Determine cloud readiness

It is not sufficient to consider only the potential *value* of moving to cloud services. Agencies should make risk-based decisions which carefully consider the *readiness* of commercial or government providers to fulfill their Federal needs. These can be wide-ranging, but likely will include: security requirements, service and marketplace characteristics, application readiness, government readiness, and program's stage in the technology lifecycle. Similar to the value estimation, agencies should be free to stress one or more of these readiness considerations according to their individual needs.

Security Requirements: Federal Government IT programs have a wide range of security requirements. Federal Information Security Management Act (FISMA) requirements include but are not limited to: compliance with Federal Information Processing Standards agency specific policies; Authorization to Operate requirements; and vulnerability and security event monitoring, logging, and reporting. It is essential that the decision to apply a specific cloud computing model to support mission capability considers these requirements. Agencies have the responsibility to ensure that a safe, secure cloud solution is available to provide a prospective IT service, and should carefully consider agency security needs across a number of dimensions, including but not limited to:

- **Statutory compliance** to laws, regulations, and agency requirements

- **Data characteristics** to assess which fundamental protections an application's data set requires

- **Privacy and confidentiality** to protect against accidental and nefarious access to information

- **Integrity** to ensure data is authorized, complete, and accurate

- **Data controls and access policies** to determine where data can be stored and who can access physical locations

- **Governance** to ensure that cloud computing service providers are sufficiently transparent, have adequate security and management controls, and provide the information necessary for the agency to appropriately and independently assess and monitor the efficacy of those controls

For additional discussion and considerations regarding trust and security in the context of cloud computing, please refer to the online NIST cloud computing resources.[10]

Service characteristics: Service characteristics can include service interoperability, availability, performance, performance measurement approaches, reliability, scalability, portability, vendor reliability, and architectural compatibility.

Storing information in the cloud will require a technical mechanism to achieve compliance with records management laws, policies and regulations promulgated by both the National Archives and Records Administration (NARA) and the General Services Administration (GSA). The cloud solution has to support relevant record safeguards and retrieval functions, even in the context of a provider termination.

Depending on the organizational missions supported by the cloud capability, Continuity of Operations (COOP) can be a driving solution requirement. The purpose of a COOP capability is to ensure that mission-essential functions continue to be available in times of crisis or against a spectrum of threats. Threats can include a wide range of potential emergencies, including localized acts of nature, accidents, and technological and/or attack-related emergencies.

The organization should consider scalability requirements concerning the ability of the cloud solution architecture to either grow or shrink over time, with varying levels of processing, storage, or service handling capability. They should also consider both the impact on their business processes if network connectivity to their cloud provider fails, resulting in a loss of IT capability, and the possibility (likelihood) of this occurrence.

Requirements concerning administrative support should be included as well, covering topics such as the daily hours of prime support, problem escalation times, resolution of recurring problems, and trouble ticket submission methods.

Market Characteristics: Agencies should consider the cloud market competitive landscape and maturity, including both fully commercial and government-provided cloud services. Agencies can consider whether cloud markets are sufficiently competitive and are not dominated by a small number of players. Agencies can consider whether there is a demonstrated capability to move services from one provider

---

10. http://csrc.nist.gov/groups/SNS/cloud-computing/
http://www.nist.gov/itl/cloud%20index.cfm

to another, and whether there is a demonstrated capability to distribute services between two or more providers in response to service quality and capacity. Agencies should consider the availability of technical standards for cloud interfaces which reduce the risk of vendor lock-in.

Network infrastructure, application and data readiness: Before migrating to the cloud agencies must ensure that the network infrastructure can support the demand for higher bandwidth and that there is sufficient redundancy for mission critical applications. Agencies should update their continuity of operations plans to reflect the increased importance of a high-bandwidth connection to the Internet or service provider. Another key factor to assess when determining readiness for migration to the cloud is the suitability of the existing legacy application and data to either migrate to the cloud (i.e., rehost an application in a cloud environment) or be replaced by a cloud service (i.e., retire the legacy system and replace with commercial SaaS equivalent). If the candidate application has clearly articulated and understood interfaces and business rules, and has limited and simple coupling with other systems and databases, it is a good candidate along this dimension. If the application has years of accumulated and poorly documented business rules embedded in code, and a proliferation of subtle or poorly understood interdependencies with other systems, the risks of "breakage" when the legacy application is migrated or retired make this a less attractive choice for early cloud adoption.

Government readiness: In addition, agencies should consider whether or not the applicable organization is pragmatically ready to migrate their service to the cloud. Government services which have capable and reliable managers, the ability to negotiate appropriate SLAs, related technical experience, and supportive change management cultures should receive a relatively high priority. Government services which do not possess these characteristics but are otherwise strong cloud candidates should take steps to alleviate any identified concerns as a matter of priority.

Technology lifecycle: Agencies should also consider where technology services (and the underlying computing assets) are in their lifecycle. Services that are nearing a technology refresh, approaching the conclusion of their negotiated contract, or are dependent upon inefficient legacy software or hardware should receive a relatively high priority. Technology services that were recently upgraded, locked within contract, and are based on leading-edge technology may want to wait before migrating to the cloud.

2. Provisioning cloud services effectively

To effectively provision selected IT services, agencies will need to rethink their processes as provisioning services rather than simply contracting assets. Contracts that previously focused on metrics such as number of servers and network bandwidth now should focus on the quality of service fulfillment.

Organizations that are most successful in cloud service provisioning carefully think through a number of factors, including:

Aggregate demand: When considering "commodity" and common IT services, agencies should pool their purchasing power by aggregating demand to the greatest extent possible before migrating services to the cloud. Where appropriate, demand should be aggregated at the departmental level and as part of the government-wide shared services initiatives such as government-wide cloud-based email.

Integrate services: Agencies should ensure that the provided IT services are effectively integrated into their wider application portfolio. In some cases, technical experts may be required to evaluate architectural compatibility of the provided cloud service and other critical applications. Rather than a one-time event, this principle should be followed over time to guarantee that systems remain interoperable as individual IT services evolve within the portfolio. Business process change may similarly be required to properly integrate the systems (e.g., adjusting call center processes).

Contract effectively: Agencies should also ensure that their contracts with cloud service providers set the service up for success. Agencies should minimize the risk of vendor lock-in, for instance, to ensure portability and encourage competition among providers. Agencies should include explicit service level agreements (SLAs) for security, continuity of operations, and service quality that meet their individual needs. Agencies should include a contractual clause enabling third parties to assess security controls of cloud providers. The SLA should specify the support steps that the consumer can take when the service is failing to meet the terms specified in the agreement, and should include points-of-contact and escalation procedures. It is important to be precise in the definition of metrics and specify when and where they will be collected. For example, performance is different when measured from the consumer or provider due to the network delays. Metrics should measure characteristics under the control of the vendor. Finally, the SLA should describe a mutual management process for the service levels, including periodic reporting requirements and meetings for management assessments.

Realize value: Agencies should take steps during migration to ensure that they fully realize the expected value. From an efficiency standpoint, legacy applications and servers should be shut down and decommissioned or repurposed. Data center real estate used to support these systems should be closed down or used to support higher value-add activities. Where possible, staff supporting these systems should be trained and re-deployed to higher-value activities. From an agility and innovation standpoint, processes and capabilities may also need to be refined in order to fully capture the value of the investment.

3. Managing services rather than assets

To be successful, agencies must manage cloud services differently than traditional IT assets. As with provisioning, cloud computing will require a new way of thinking to reflect a service-based focus rather than an asset-based focus. Listed below are a few considerations for agencies to effectively manage their cloud services.

Shift mindset: Organizations need to re-orient the focus of all parties involved – providers, government agencies, and end users – to think of services rather than assets. Organizations that successfully make this transition will effectively manage the system towards output metrics (e.g., SLAs) rather than input metrics (e.g., number of servers).

Actively monitor: Agencies should actively track SLAs and hold vendors accountable for failures. Agencies should stay ahead of emerging security threats and ensure that their security outlook is constantly evolving faster than potential attacks. Agencies may also consider incorporating business user feedback into evaluation processes. Finally, agencies should track usage rates to ensure charges do not exceed funded amounts.

It can be advantageous for a consumer to "instrument" key points on the network to measure performance of cloud service providers. For example, commercial tools can report back to a centralized data store on service performance, and instrumentation agents can be placed with participating consumers and at the entry point of the service provider on the network. By gathering data across providers on the performance of pre-planned instrumented service calls throughout typical work periods, service managers can better judge where performance bottlenecks arise. Agencies should include requirements for service instrumentation where appropriate.

Re-evaluate periodically: Agencies should periodically re-evaluate the choice of service and vendor to ensure that efficiency, agility, and innovation are maximized. Agencies should ensure portability and hold competitive bids for cloud services at regular intervals. Agencies should also consider increasing the scope of cloud-provided services as markets mature (e.g., moving from IaaS solutions to PaaS and SaaS solutions). Opportunities to consolidate and standardize solutions between agencies should be periodically evaluated as well, particularly for "commodity" services. To effectively conduct re-evaluations, agencies should maintain awareness of changes in the technology landscape, in particular, the readiness of new cloud technologies, commercial innovation, and new cloud vendors.

III. CASE EXAMPLES TO ILLUSTRATE FRAMEWORK

Many Federal agencies have already taken their first steps towards cloud computing. In each case, the agency achieved considerable benefits to efficiency, agility, or innovation in support of its unique mission. The following case studies illustrate how these Federal agencies successfully migrated toward cloud services consistent with the select / provision / manage framework outlined in Section 2.

1. Tailoring solution to protect security and maximize value

In 2008, the Army Experience Center (AEC) realized that it needed a new Customer Relationship Management (CRM) system to track personal and electronic engagements with prospects and help recruiting staff manage the recruitment process.

After considering several options including upgrading their 10-year-old legacy proprietary data system, the Army chose a customized version of a commercially-available SaaS solution. This solution met their unique security needs, fulfilled all of their functionality requirements, and was delivered at a fraction of the time and expense required to upgrade their legacy system.

The Army followed many of the key factors outlined in Section 2 when migrating toward their cloud solution:

Selecting a cloud solution

The Army placed a very high priority on security when considering its CRM solution. Before choosing a cloud solution, the AEC carefully weighed the sources of value and readiness of potential solutions.

Efficiency: The AEC compared the cost of upgrading their existing system to configuring a new SaaS solution. Initial bids to upgrade the existing system, ARISS, which relied on traditional infrastructure, ranged from $500,000 to over $1 million. Initial pilots of the SaaS solution cost as little as $54,000, just over 10% of the minimum cost of an ARISS system upgrade.

Agility: The AEC also considered the time required to deploy the system. Despite regular upgrades over the years, it was infeasible to modify ARISS to meet the Army Experience Center's requirements. The SaaS solution could be provisioned in a fraction of the time required to upgrade the ARISS system. The SaaS solution was also more scalable and would be far easier to upgrade over time.

Innovation: The SaaS solution integrated directly with e-mail and Facebook, allowing recruiters to connect with participants more dynamically after they left the AEC. Army recruiters could also access information from anywhere. These advancements would have been very costly and time-consuming to achieve with ARISS system upgrades. In effect, the SaaS solution allowed the AEC to take advantage of the cloud vendor's innovation engine without owning or managing heavy IT assets.

Security: The AEC ensured the cloud solution would be sufficiently secure. The SaaS solution was flexible and could be configured to securely manage access, sovereignty, and data retention requirements.

Market availability: The SaaS solution was able to meet all of the AEC's requirements including the ability to track AEC visitor and engagement data, compatibility with handheld devices, and real-time integration with marketing and recruitment data.

Government readiness: The AEC ensured that it was both capable and ready to migrate their services to the cloud. The AEC had experience implementing new technologies, had a culture that supported experimentation and improvement, and possessed the skills and capacity to manage the transition well.

Technology lifecycle: The AEC also evaluated the lifecycle of its legacy solution. The legacy ARISS system was more than 10 years old in 2008 and was not burdened by contract lock-down.

Provisioning IT services

During provisioning, the AEC took an approach which was distinctly different from the Army's former approach with ARISS. This approach reflected the service-based rather than asset-based nature of the cloud service.

Integrate services: As the Army transferred its recruitment system to the cloud, it carefully engineered its relationship with the vendor to ensure a successful migration.

Realize value: With the cloud-based solution, the AEC has been able to handle the workload of five traditional recruitment centers. The system has also resulted in dramatically reduced hardware costs and IT staff costs. The Army has decommissioned, or re-purposed for other systems, all hardware related to the legacy ARISS system. Its people have been spending more time on more rewarding and higher-value activities, shifting time from filing reports to engaging with potential recruits.

2. Provisioning to ensure competitiveness and capture value

USDA recently launched a broad initiative to modernize and streamline USDA's IT infrastructure. As part of this initiative, USDA aimed to consolidate 21 fragmented e-mail systems and improve the productivity of its workers. Rather than continuing efforts to consolidate the fragmented environment internally, the USDA chose a proven cloud-based email solution to accelerate consolidation and take advantage of the latest communication and collaboration tools.

Effective provisioning was critical for the USDA to realize the value of cloud migration. Previously, the USDA had focused on contracting for its 21 email systems. As a provisioner, the USDA needed to carefully aggregate demand, ensure integration with downstream applications, reflect its priorities in its contracts, and retire legacy systems to capture value.

The USDA followed many of the key factors outlined in Section 2 when migrating toward their cloud solution:

Selecting a cloud solution

The USDA carefully evaluated the sources of value and service readiness before choosing the cloud-based solution:

Efficiency: Financially, the motivation to move to cloud was compelling. Eliminating the 21 fragmented e-mail systems would drastically reduce duplication, not only with software and hardware assets, but also by reducing the number of system interfaces that need to be maintained on a regular basis. USDA estimates that the cloud solution will save up to $6 million per year, to include ongoing costs for hardware refreshment and software upgrades.

Agility: Consolidating and upgrading their fragmented traditional environment would have taken years to complete. With the cloud solution, USDA was able to access the cloud provider's existing capacity to accommodate its 120,000 users. Migration would require months rather than years. Once complete, the solution would be more scalable to the needs of USDA.

Innovation: The cloud solution allowed USDA to make the latest communication and collaboration tools available to its workers including SharePoint, Office Communications, and Live Meeting online services. In addition, USDA was able to incorporate e-discovery and archive features.

Market availability: The functionality offered by the cloud solution met the needs of USDA. The cloud provider also had experience hosting very large email systems, including 300,000 users from a large private sector client. Cloud-provided e-mail is a vibrant, competitive market with several capable market incumbents.

Government readiness: Senior leadership was actively involved and highly motivated to improve the efficiency and quality of the email services. The USDA CIO was personally involved in many of the decisions. The broader transformation program also provided valuable delivery resources to execute the migration.

Technology lifecycle: The 21 email systems were approaching the end of their usable lifecycle and were not burdened by inflexible contracts.

Provisioning IT services

USDA's provisioning approach reflected a service-based mindset rather than an asset-based mindset.

Aggregate demand: USDA implemented their cloud email solution on an agency-wide level. This approach maximized benefits and addressed their primary, fundamental concern – fragmented email systems. The approach also allowed USDA to take full advantage of the momentum created by the broader transformation agenda.

Integrate services: An auxiliary contract was awarded to a systems integrator to ensure the e-mail system was properly integrated with the various interfacing USDA systems. Seven hundred applications reliant upon email were analyzed – only four had to be recoded to maintain operations.

Contract effectively: USDA benchmarked their cloud provider against the industry to ensure competitive market rates. USDA also embedded explicit SLAs into the contract, according to its mission needs.

Realize value: Previously used IT assets are on track to be decommissioned and/or re-deployed as part of the wider IT modernization strategy. Individuals formerly working on email have been reassigned to higher-value projects and activities, with some continuing to coordinate service delivery of email.

Managing cloud services

USDA has revised its management approach to reflect a service-based rather than asset-based mindset.

Build new management skills: USDA built up its contract management and performance management capabilities to support the new cloud environment. USDA also relied on a system integrator to temporarily provide the skills and expertise to successfully complete the migration.

Active monitoring: USDA will continuously monitor the SLAs outlined in their cloud service contract. This includes security issues such as domestic storage of data and performance metrics such as minimum uptime, recovery speed, and bandwidth latency.

3. Re-defining IT from an asset to a service

The Defense Information Systems Agency (DISA) provides global infrastructure services to support US and coalition fighting forces. To better meet the needs of defense-related computing needs domestically and in the field, DISA decided to deploy its own Infrastructure-as-a-Service (IaaS) solution.

DISA's Rapid Access Computing Environment (RACE) has redefined defense infrastructure from an asset management function to a service provisioning function. Since the inception of the cloud-based solution, hundreds of military applications including command and control systems, convoy control systems, and satellite programs have been developed and tested on RACE.

DISA followed many of the key factors outlined in Section 2 when implementing their cloud solution:

Selecting a cloud solution

DISA determined that a private IaaS solution would realize the desired improvements in efficiency, agility, and innovation while maintaining strict security controls.

Efficiency: RACE has been able to reach higher utilization levels through cloud technologies than previously available via traditional infrastructure by aggregating demand and thus smoothing out peak loads. These improvements in utilization divide the costs of provisioning and operating infrastructure among a broader group of consumers.

Agility: Using traditional infrastructure, provisioning a dedicated server environment required 3 to 6 weeks. With RACE, the time required to provision functional service space for users is now 24 hours.

Security: RACE has built-in application separation controls so that all applications, databases, and web servers are separate from each other. DISA also has a strict cleansing process, to be used when an application needs to be removed from the RACE platform.

Managing cloud services

As DoD organizations obtain infrastructure through RACE, they are able to shift focus toward software design while interfacing with RACE staff through SLAs.

Shift mindset: RACE has actively encouraged a service-based mindset from its users. DISA created a self-service portal through which users can provision services in 50GB increments through a government credit card. Project and software designers have increasingly used RACE to meet their infrastructure needs rather than relying on custom infrastructure configurations.

Build new management skills: DISA built new capabilities to support their operations. On the supply side, a single operational manager is ultimately responsible for meeting cost and performance metrics. A new demand manager has also been added to solicit, prioritize, and coordinate user needs for service improvements.

Actively monitor: DISA monitors and continuously improves a number of SLAs focused on service quality. Performance dashboards include average and maximum wait times for provisioning services in the field.

Re-evaluate periodically: Less than one year after launching the IaaS service, DISA announced that it would provide private SaaS services, such as the RightNow installation for the Air Force.

IV. CATALYZING CLOUD ADOPTION

As agencies develop plans to migrate services to cloud computing options, there are a number of activities that Federal Government leadership can take to facilitate adoption and mitigate risk. Cloud computing "accelerators," described below, can help improve the pace of evaluating candidate services and acquisitions. Government-wide Certification and Accreditation (C&A) and security efforts at the Department of Homeland Security (DHS) and NIST can help agencies efficiently acquire cloud computing capabilities and mitigate threats. Procurement efforts can be streamlined through the use of government-wide procurement vehicles and storefronts such as those found at Apps.gov. Further, NIST is driving a standards effort that is focused on requirements to ensure security, interoperability, and portability among cloud service providers.

1. Leveraging cloud computing accelerators

Cloud computing accelerators are resources available to agencies to expedite the process of evaluating cloud candidates, acquiring the cloud capability, and mitigating risk.[11]

Cloud computing business case templates and examples

The Federal CIO Council has developed cloud computing business cases and will continue to build this library to support agencies in their cloud computing decisions.

Agencies should seek out business cases of similar scope or purpose to speed up the development of their own cloud computing business cases (e.g., decision criteria for moving cloud email, cloud CRM, cloud storage).

Government cloud computing community and resources

Agencies should participate in government cloud computing working groups at NIST and GSA on topics such as standards, reference architecture, taxonomy, security, privacy and business use cases.[12] Agencies can also leverage portals, such as NIST's Collaboration site, which provides access to useful information for cloud adopters.[13] More cloud computing resources are included in Appendix 2.

Despite the resources discussed above, agencies may face a number of issues that can impede their ability to fully realize the benefits from a cloud computing approach. As in the case of all technology advancement, these challenges will change over time, as the cloud computing marketplace evolves. In the near-term, organizations within the Federal Government, including OMB, NIST, GSA, and DHS, have developed and continue to develop practical guidance on issues related to security, procurement, and standards and are establishing the governance foundation required to support delivery.

---

11. Adopted from Raines and Pizette, *A Decision Process for Applying Cloud Computing in Federal Environments*, 2010
12. http://collaborate.nist.gov/twiki-cloud-computing/bin/view/CloudComputing/WebHome, http://www.info.apps.gov/node/2
13. http://collaborate.nist.gov/twiki-cloud-computing/bin/view/CloudComputing/WebHome

2. Ensuring a secure, trustworthy environment

As the Federal Government moves to the cloud, it must be vigilant to ensure the security and proper management of government information to protect the privacy of citizens and national security.

The transition to outsourced, cloud computing environment is in many ways an exercise in risk management. Risk management entails identifying and assessing risk, and taking the steps to reduce it to an acceptable level. Throughout the system lifecycle, risks that are identified must be carefully balanced against the security and privacy controls available and the expected benefits. Too many controls can be inefficient and ineffective. Federal agencies and organizations should work to ensure an appropriate balance between the number and strength of controls and the risks associated with cloud computing solutions.

The Federal Government will create a transparent security environment between cloud providers and cloud consumers. The environment will move us to a level where the Federal Government's understanding and ability to assess its security posture will be superior to what is provided within agencies today. The first step in this process was the 2010 Federal Risk and Authorization Management Program (FedRAMP). FedRAMP defined requirements for cloud computing security controls, including vulnerability scanning, and incident monitoring, logging and reporting.[14] Implementing these controls will improve confidence and encourage trust in the cloud computing environment.

To strengthen security from an operational perspective, DHS will prioritize a list of top security threats every 6 months or as needed, and work with a government-wide team of security experts to ensure that proper security controls and measures are implemented to mitigate these threats.

NIST will issue technical security guidance,[15] such as that focused on continuous monitoring for cloud computing solutions, consistent with the six step Risk Management Framework (Special Publication 800-37, Revision 1).[16]

---

14. http://www.fedramp.gov
15. Ref. National Institute of Standards and Technology (NIST) statutory responsibilities for developing standards and guidelines, Federal Information Security Management Act (FISMA) of 2002, Public Law 107-347
16. http://www.nist.gov/itl/csd/guide_030210.cfm

Figure 5: NIST Risk Management Framework

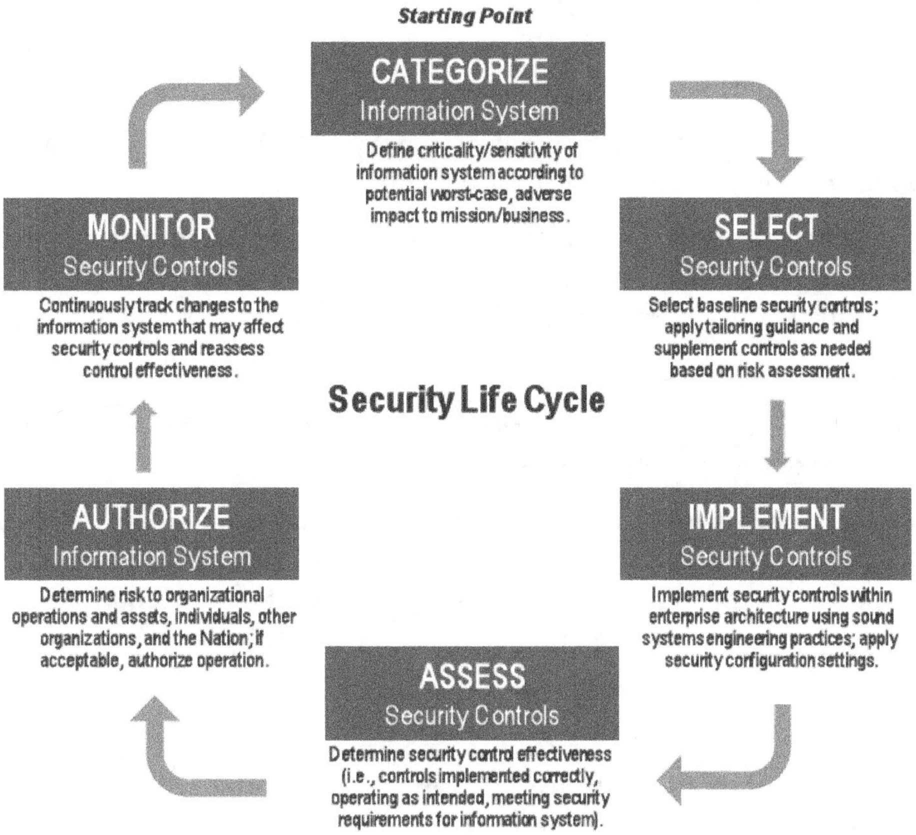

Starting Point

CATEGORIZE
Information System

Define criticality/sensitivity of information system according to potential worst-case, adverse impact to mission/business.

MONITOR
Security Controls

Continuously track changes to the information system that may affect security controls and reassess control effectiveness.

SELECT
Security Controls

Select baseline security controls; apply tailoring guidance and supplement controls as needed based on risk assessment.

Security Life Cycle

AUTHORIZE
Information System

Determine risk to organizational operations and assets, individuals, other organizations, and the Nation; if acceptable, authorize operation.

IMPLEMENT
Security Controls

Implement security controls within enterprise architecture using sound systems engineering practices; apply security configuration settings.

ASSESS
Security Controls

Determine security control effectiveness (i.e., controls implemented correctly, operating as intended, meeting security requirements for information system).

Agencies assessing risk in the context of cloud computing should consider both the potential security benefits and potential vulnerabilities.

Potential security benefits of using cloud computing services include:

- **the ability to focus resources** on areas of high concern as more general security services are assumed by the cloud provider

- **potential platform strength** resulting from greater uniformity and homogeneity, and resulting improved information assurance, security response, system management, reliability, and maintainability

- **improved resource availability** through scalability, redundancy and disaster recovery capabilities; improved resilience to unanticipated service demands

- **improved backup and recovery** capabilities, policies, procedures and consistency

- **ability to leverage alternate cloud services** to improve the overall security posture, including that of traditional data centers

Agencies should also weigh the additional potential vulnerabilities associated with various cloud computing service and deployment models, such as:

- **the inherent system complexity** of a cloud computing environment, and the dependency on the correctness of these components and the interactions among them

- **the dependency on the service provider to maintain logical separation in a multi-tenant environment** (n.b., not unique to the cloud computing model)

- **the need to ensure that the organization retains an appropriate level of control** to obtain situational awareness, weigh alternatives, set priorities, and effect changes in security and privacy that are in the best interest of the organization

Key security considerations include the need to:

- **carefully define security and privacy requirements** during the initial planning stage at the start of the systems development life cycle

- **determine the extent to which negotiated service agreements are required** to satisfy security requirements; and the alternatives of using negotiated service agreements or cloud computing deployment models which offer greater oversight and control over security and privacy

- **assess the extent to which the server and client-side computing environment** meets organizational security and privacy requirements

- **continue to maintain security management** practices, controls, and accountability over the privacy and security of data and applications

In the short and long-term, these actions will continue to improve our confidence in the use of cloud services by helping to mitigate security risks.

3. Streamlining procurement processes

Currently, the government often purchases commodities in a fragmented non-aggregated fashion, operating more like a federation of small businesses than an $80 billion enterprise. To improve readiness for cloud computing, the Federal Government will facilitate an "approve once and use often" approach to streamline the approval process for cloud service providers. For instance, a government-wide risk and authorization program for IaaS solutions will allow agencies to rely on existing authorizations so only additional, agency-specific requirements will need to be authorized separately. The GSA's IaaS contract award is an example of this "approve once and use often" approach. It offers 12 approved cloud vendors to provide agencies with cloud storage, virtual machines, and web hosting services. Approaches such as this will eliminate unnecessary cost and delivery delays associated with duplication of effort.

As the number of government cloud providers increases, GSA will provide comparison tools to transparently compare cloud providers side-by-side. These tools will allow agencies to quickly and effectively select the best offering for their unique needs. Examples include Apps.gov, which provides a centralized storefront where agencies can easily browse and compare cloud SaaS and IaaS offerings from previous

Multiple Award Schedule (MAS) 70 contract holders. Tools such as these will reduce the burden on agencies to conduct their own RFP processes and will concentrate investments in the highest-performing cloud providers.

Furthermore, GSA will establish contract vehicles for government-wide commodity services (e.g., email). These contract vehicles will reduce the burden on agencies for the most common IT services. GSA will also create working groups to support commodity service migration. These working groups will develop technical requirements for shared services to reduce the analytical burden on individual government agencies. For example, the SaaS E-mail working group established in June 2010 is synthesizing requirements for government-wide e-mail services. Working groups will also create business case templates for agencies that are considering transitioning to cloud technologies.

Federal Government contracts will also provide riders for state and local governments. These riders will allow all of these governments to realize the same procurement advantages of the Federal Government. Increasing membership in cloud services will further drive innovation and cost efficiency by increasing market size and creating larger efficiencies-of-scale.

4. Establishing cloud computing standards

Standards will be critical for the successful adoption and delivery of cloud computing, both within the public sector and more broadly. Standards encourage competition by making applications portable across providers, allowing Federal agencies to shift services between providers to take advantage of cost efficiency improvements or innovative new product functionality. Standards are also critical to ensure clouds have an interoperable platform so that services provided by different providers can work together, regardless of whether they are provided using public, private, community, or a hybrid delivery model.

NIST will play a central role in defining standards, and collaborating with Agency CIOs, private sector experts, and international bodies to identify, prioritize, and reach consensus on standardization priorities.[17] In 2010, NIST conducted engagement workshops to identify and prioritize needs. Going forward, NIST will generate, assess, and revise a cloud computing roadmap on a periodic basis. This roadmap will iteratively define and track the agreed-upon cloud computing priorities in order to coordinate cloud efforts across stakeholders.

NIST will maintain a leadership role in prioritizing, developing, evolving and refining standards over time as the collective requirements for standards evolve in response to operationally driven innovation and technology evolution. NIST has already helped to establish broadly adopted definitions for the four commonly recognized cloud deployment models (i.e., private, public, hybrid, and community) and three service models (i.e., Infrastructure as a Service, Platform as a Service, and Software as a Service), as discussed in Section 1. However, these definitions need to be expanded to more comprehensively define a reference architecture and taxonomy to provide a common frame of reference for communication. NIST is currently working with industry and other cloud computing stakeholders to define a neutral reference architecture that is not tied to a specific set of vendor solutions or products or constrained in such a

---

17. Ref. National Institute of Standards and Technology (NIST) is directed to bring together Federal agencies, as well as State and local governments, to achieve greater reliance on voluntary standards and decreased dependence on in-house standards., National Technology Transfer and Advancement Act (NTTAA) 1995, Public Law 104 -113

way that it will inhibit innovation. As cloud providers create new solutions, this reference architecture will serve as the basis for an "apples to apples" comparison of cloud computing services. This will help agencies to understand how various services fit together. Similarly, NIST will need to expand these definitions as new deployment models arise.

NIST will work with agencies to define a set of "target" business use cases that pose the greatest challenges by risks, concerns, or constraints. NIST will help to identify operationally driven priorities for cloud computing standards and guidance by working with Federal agencies and other stakeholders to define a set of mission driven scenarios for cloud computing implementation and operations. These will be used to focus and help to translate mission requirements into technical portability, interoperability, reliability, maintainability and security requirements. For example, a business use case may reflect the migration of patent application software to cloud IaaS. Once identified, NIST will work with agencies and industry to model, using a vendor neutral reference architecture and taxonomy as a frame of reference, various options for addressing these challenges. Ultimately, this research will result in the definition of new standards, guidance, and technology requirements.[18]

NIST will continue to execute the tactical Standards Acceleration to Jumpstart Adoption of Cloud Computing (SAJACC) project, which plays a role in validating key cloud specifications and sharing information, in order to build confidence in cloud computing technology before formalized standards are available. To date, SAJACC has defined 24 generic technical use cases that can be used to validate key interoperability, security, and portability requirements. One example is the ability to move data in to and out of a cloud provider's environment, and to verify that data is adequately deleted when removed using commonly available interfaces defined by industry. SAJACC will support industry in moving forward with standardization in parallel with the formal consensus based standards organizations' processes.

5. Recognizing the international dimensions of cloud computing

The growth of any new technology presents two fundamental dynamics: (1) the power to transform and (2) the need to examine existing paradigms in that same field. Cloud computing has brought to the forefront several international policy issues that need to be addressed over the next decade as cloud computing matures. Issues to consider include:

- Data sovereignty, data in motion, and data access: How do countries strike the proper balance between privacy, security and intellectual property of national data?

- Are there needs for international cloud computing legal, regulatory, or governance frameworks?

- Cloud computing codes of conducts for national governments, industry, and non-governmental organizations

- Data interoperability and portability in domestic and international settings

- Ensuring global harmonization of cloud computing standards

---

18. www.nist.gov/itl/cloud/bususecases.cfm

6. Laying a solid governance foundation

This strategy is the first step in the process of migrating towards cloud technologies, both within the public and private sector. The Federal Government will play a vital role throughout this process to identify and resolve cloud issues of national importance. As issues are increasingly resolved, the Federal Government will re-focus its priorities towards more pressing issues.

To effectively manage these governance issues in the long-term, the Federal Government needs to lay a stable governance foundation that will outlast single individuals or administrations. To the best extent possible, individuals or committees should have explicitly defined roles, non-overlapping responsibilities, and a clear decision-making hierarchy. These steps will empower the government for action, minimize unnecessary bureaucracy, and ensure accountability for results.

The following bodies will therefore have these roles and responsibilities:

- *National Institute of Standards and Technology (NIST)* will lead and collaborate with Federal, State, and local government agency CIOs, private sector experts, and international bodies to identify and prioritize cloud computing standards and guidance

- *General Service Administration (GSA)* will develop government-wide procurement vehicles and develop government-wide and cloud-based application solutions where needed

- *Department of Homeland Security (DHS)* will monitor operational security issues related to the cloud

- *Agencies* will be responsible for evaluating their sourcing strategies to fully consider cloud computing solutions

- *Federal CIO Council* will drive government-wide adoption of cloud, identify next-generation cloud technologies, and share best practices and reusable example analyses and templates

- *The Office of Management and Budget (OMB)* will coordinate activities across governance bodies, set overall cloud-related priorities, and provide guidance to agencies

V. CONCLUSION

Cheaper processors, faster networks, and the rise of mobile devices are driving innovation faster than ever before. Cloud computing is a manifestation and core enabler of this transformation. Just as the Internet has led to the creation of new business models unfathomable 20 years ago, cloud computing will disrupt and reshape entire industries in unforeseen ways. To paraphrase Sir Arthur Eddington – the physicist who confirmed Einstein's *Theory of General Relativity* – cloud computing will not just be more innovative than we imagine; it will be more innovative than we *can* imagine.

IDC predicted that by this year, the digital universe would be 10 times the size it was in 2006 – that is, nine times more digital content would be created within five years than all of history before.[19] This explosion of data, combined with the mobilization of digital access, portends major improvements in on-the-go intelligence. Examples of transformative changes exist across all government agencies and it is the responsibility of those in government to be in the forefront of bringing these innovative services to the American people. It is very easy to envision new services such as personalized flu outbreak warnings for expectant mothers and real-time traffic advisories performed by Federal and local governments.

Cloud computing will enable a fundamental shift in how we serve the American people. Citizens empowered to see their homes' electricity use in real-time will be able to make more intelligent consumption choices. Citizens able to access their health records electronically will be able to easily share them with doctors and providers, and thus improve their healthcare. Citizens able to create and share performance dashboards will be able to shine a light on the government's performance as easily as they create and share YouTube videos today.

Our responsibility in government is to achieve the significant cost, agility and innovation benefits of cloud computing as quickly as possible. The strategy and actions described in this paper are the means for us to get started immediately. Given that each agency has unique mission needs, security requirements, and IT landscape, we ask that each agency think through the attached strategy as a next step. Each agency will evaluate its technology sourcing strategy so that cloud computing options are fully considered, consistent with the Cloud First policy.

---

19. Gantz, John. *The Diverse and Exploding Digital Universe: An Updated Forecast on Worldwide Information Growth through 2011.* March 2008

APPENDIX 1: POTENTIAL SPENDING ON CLOUD COMPUTING BY AGENCY

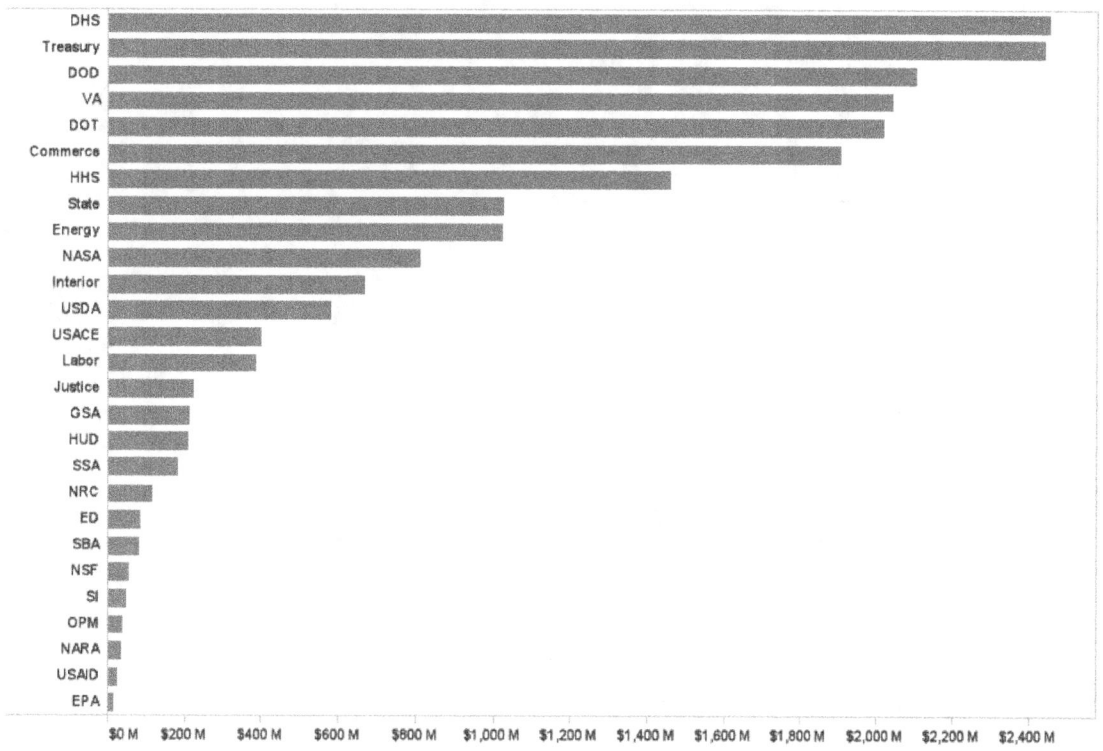

Source: Agency estimates reported to the Office of Management and Budget (OMB).

APPENDIX 2: AGENCY RESOURCES FOR CLOUD COMPUTING

General

- **The ABCs of Cloud Computing:** A comprehensive cloud computing portal where agencies can get information on procurement, security, best practices, case studies and technical resources. (GSA / http://www.info.apps.gov)

- **Cloud Computing Migration Framework:** A series of technical white papers on cloud computing, including a decision-making framework, cost/business case considerations, service level agreement provisions, information security, a PaaS analysis and a survey of market segments and cloud products categories. (MITRE / http://www.mitre.org/work/info_tech/cloud_computing/technical_papers/index.html)

- **Successful Case Studies:** A report which details 30 illustrative cloud computing case studies at the Federal, state and local government levels. (CIO Council / http://www.info.apps.gov/sites/default/files/StateOfCloudComputingReport-FINALv3_508.pdf)

- **Cloud Computing Definition:** Includes essential characteristics as well as service and deployment models. (NIST / http://csrc.nist.gov/publications/drafts/800-145/Draft-SP-800-145_cloud-definition.pdf)

Security

- **Centralized Cloud Computing Assessment and Authorization:** The Federal Risk and Authorization Management Program (FedRAMP) has been established to provide a standard, centralized approach to assessing and authorizing cloud computing services and products. FedRAMP will permit joint authorizations and continuous security monitoring services for government and commercial cloud computing systems intended for multi-agency use. It will enable the government to buy a cloud solution once, but use it many times. (CIO Council / http://www.fedramp.gov)

- **Primer on Cloud Computing Security:** A white paper that seeks to clarify the variations of cloud services and examine the current and near-term potential for Federal cloud computing from a cybersecurity perspective. (DHS / http://www.info.apps.gov/sites/default/files/Cloud_Computing_Security_Perspective.doc)

- **Privacy Recommendations for Cloud Computing:** A paper which highlights potential privacy risks agencies should consider as they migrate to cloud computing (CIO Council / http://www.cio.gov/Documents/Privacy-Recommendations-Cloud-Computing-8-19-2010.docx)

- **Guide for Applying the Risk Management Framework to Federal Information Systems, A Security Life Cycle Approach** (NIST / http://csrc.nist.gov/publications/nistpubs/800-37-rev1/sp800-37-rev1-final.pdf)

- **Guidelines on Security and Privacy in Public Cloud Computing:** This draft publication provides an overview of the security and privacy challenges pertinent to public cloud computing and points out considerations organizations should take when outsourcing data, applications, and infrastructure to a public cloud environment (NIST / http://csrc.nist.gov/publications/drafts/800-144/Draft-SP-800-144_cloud-computing.pdf)

Acquisition/Procurement

- **Cloud Computing Procurement Assistance:** Apps.gov is an online cloud computing (SaaS, IaaS, PaaS) storefront that encourages and enable the adoption of cloud computing solutions across the Federal Government. Apps.gov offers a comprehensive set of business, infrastructure, productivity and social media applications. It eliminates unnecessary research, analysis and redundant approvals, requisitions and service level agreements across the government by providing agencies a fast, easy way to buy the tools they need. (GSA / https://apps.gov/)

Standards

- **Federal Cloud Computing Collaboration Page:** The National Institute of Standards and Technology (NIST) has been designated by the Federal CIO to accelerate the Federal Government's secure adoption of cloud computing by leading efforts to develop standards and guidelines in close consultation and collaboration with standards bodies, the private sector, and other stakeholders. This site provides an avenue for interested stakeholders to collaborate with NIST in developing interoperability, portability and security standards, business and technical use cases, and a cloud computing reference architecture and taxonomy. (http://collaborate.nist.gov/twiki-cloud-computing/bin/view/CloudComputing/WebHome)

Technical Resources

- **CIO Council Executive Cloud Computing Executive Steering Committee (CCESC):** The CCESC was established by the Federal CIO Council to provide strategic direction and oversight for the Federal Cloud Computing Initiative. Under the CCESC, there exists a Cloud Computing Advisory Council and multiple working groups that further enable the adoption of cloud computing across the government. (Chaired by USAID)

  - CIO Council Cloud Computing Advisory Council (CCAC): The CCAC was established at the behest of the CCESC to serve as a collaborative environment for senior IT experts from across the Federal Government. CCAC members serve as agency resources best practices dissemination, consensus building for key Federal Cloud Computing initiatives, and the sharing of existing/planned cloud computing projects. (Chaired by USAID)

- CIO Council Cloud Computing E-mail Working Group: The E-mail Working Group will be the source of SaaS email information, solutions, and processes that foster adoption of SaaS email across the Federal Government. (Chaired by DOI)

- CIO Council Cloud Computing Security Working Group: The Security Working Group supports FedRAMP, a centralized cloud computing assessment and authorization body that can be leveraged by multiple agencies. (Chaired by GSA)

- CIO Council Cloud Computing Standards Working Group: The Standards Working Group will lead government-wide efforts to define cloud computing security, portability and interoperability standards, target Federal business and technical use cases, and a reference architecture. (Chaired by NIST)

Additional workgroups will be stood up by the CIO Council as the work of the Federal Cloud Computing Initiative evolves.